# the *SuperNatural Dessert Cookbook*
## a book of *unreal* desserts

*written by Lois Fishkin*
*illustrations & script by Susan DiMarco*

**CREATIVE ARTS BOOK COMPANY**
BERKELEY • 1984

...also by the authors:

THE NOT-STRICTLY VEGETARIAN COOKBOOK

FROM THE HOUSE AT POOH CORNER by A.A. Milne, Copyright 1928 by E.P. Dutton & Co., Inc., renewed 1956 by A.A. Milne. Reprinted by permission of the publisher.

Copyright © 1984 by Lois Fishkin and Susan DiMarco.

All rights reserved. No part of this book may be used or reproduced in any manner whatsoever without written permission from the publisher, except in the case of brief quotations embodied in articles or reviews.

For information, address the publisher:
CREATIVE ARTS BOOK COMPANY
833 BANCROFT WAY
BERKELEY, CALIFORNIA 94710

Creative Arts Books are published by:
Donald S. Ellis

ISBN 0-916870-61-8
LIBRARY OF CONGRESS CATALOG CARD NO. 84-45095

*We'd like to thank ...*

... Don Ellis, our publisher, the Great Kahuna — whose support and relentless pressure has made this book what it is today

... Harris and Ricky, for being there — and for holding down the fort

... our families, for their love and support, and for helping with the children — and special thanks to Mimi, Amy & Nana Jean

... Richard, for his invaluable editing expertise and feedback

... Sheryl, for her proofreading and critiquing skills

... Annie, for her great one-liners and <u>newly</u>-found literary contributions

... Penny, for always lending an ear, and understanding

... and, all our other friends, for sharing their <u>best</u>

# INTRODUCTION

It could be said that natural desserts have a bad name. Though some people know just how delectable such dainties can be, many people grimace at the mere mention of "natural." Why is that so? Think about it: You may remember the first time you tasted a carob brownie. It didn't look very fudgie, but you overlooked that, and you even ignored the fact that it looked a bit on the dry side. However, keeping an open mind, you took a bite, only to find that it <u>was</u> dry, somewhat gritty, only vaguely sweet, and nothing like any respectable brownie you ever tasted! Was it a <u>dessert</u>??

So, it was <u>good</u> for you. Was that reason enough to eat it? Who really cares if it's made with wheat germ, carob and tofu? You want a dessert that tastes <u>good</u>!

Remember when you were a child, and you choked down your dinner so that you could get to dessert? Dessert conjures up the feeling of reward, comfort, sweet pleasure. Of <u>course</u> we balk at the suggestion that these bland "natural" concoctions can replace our beloved delights. We <u>can't</u> be blamed for loving chocolate!! Whether we only live once is <u>not</u> the question. The question <u>is</u>, what about chocolate mousse...? (or a symbolic substitute!) Maybe chocolate mousse is too limited. What about chocolate puddings, cakes, cookies, icings, pies, chips, and even chocolate milk? Is chocolate the only way... or can comfort really be found in a natural dessert?

That is where this book comes in. We too, have suffered disappointment with natural desserts, but we didn't give up. We always believed that natural should in fact be <u>better</u>, since the ingredients used are the finest, freshest, and purest available. You can't always compromise; some desserts just cannot be made without sugar, processed flour, etc. We are not purists ourselves. We will confess to thoroughly enjoying an occasional (sometimes frequent) rich, rich, rich piece of chocolate whatever, and we can't count the many times we have soothed our frazzled souls with hot fudge sundaes.

But alas, we must balance our indulgences and our disciplines. We cannot eat chocolate all the time without suffering for it. Moderation is a word we all have come to respect. So here we all are, trying to improve our diets without sacrificing pleasure. For some, life without chocolate will always be dismal, but we offer you this book, full of delectables that satisfy... <u>truly</u> satisfy.

Yes, it is possible to have your cake and eat it, too!

## TABLE OF CONTENTS

Pies, Cobblers, Crisps, etc. ..................... 1

Cakes, Cookies, Brownies, etc. .............. 35

Muffins, Crusts, Fritters, etc. ............. 65

Puddings, and everything else ............. 87

Glossary ............................................... 103

Index ..................................................... 111

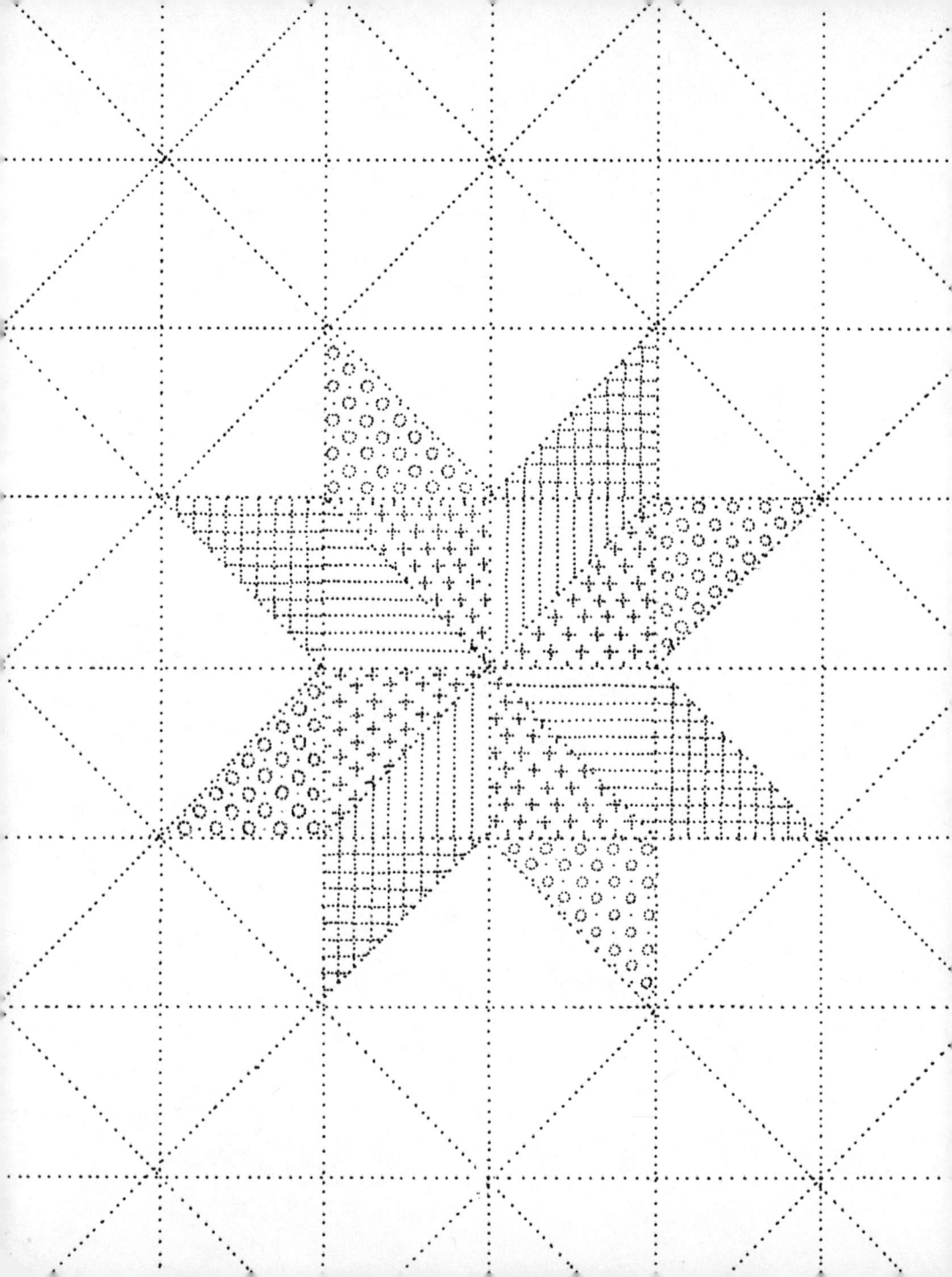

# Pies, Cobblers, Crisps, etc.

Pumpkin Apple Pie ............................................. 2
Creamy Peach Berry Pie ..................................... 4
Strawberry Rhubarb Sublime ............................. 6
Pumpkin Cream Pie ............................................ 8
Pecan Pie ........................................................... 10
Apple Walnut Crunch ....................................... 12
Sour Cherry Kuchen ......................................... 14
Nectar-Berry Pie ............................................... 16
Crumb Top Peach Pie ....................................... 18
Strawberry Cream Pie ...................................... 20
Peach Cobbler ................................................... 22
Divine Apple Cream Torte ................................ 24
Honey Glazed Blueberry Tart ........................... 26
Mango Mania .................................................... 28
Crumble Berry Pie ............................................ 30
Black Raspberry Crisp ...................................... 32
Punk-In Pie ....................................................... 33

# Pumpkin Apple Pie

*... a great combination — total harmony!*

I used a fresh pumpkin squash that I kept in a cool place over the winter... peeled, cooked & pureed it in the spring, and it yielded 6 qts. of pumpkin. I froze individual servings... it can also be put up in mason jars. All in all, it was very inexpensive.... and the flavor far surpasses commercially canned pumpkin.

### CRUST:

- 1½ cups whole wheat pastry flour
- ½ cup finely chopped walnuts
- 1 stick butter
- 3 tbsp. water

### FILLING:

- 2 cups pureed pumpkin
- 8 oz. cream cheese
- 4 lg. apples (I used MacIntosh... peeled, cored and chopped)
- 2 lg. eggs

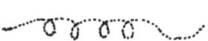

1 cup maple syrup
juice of 1 orange
3 tbsp. cinnamon (I *love* cinnamon!)
1 tsp. allspice
½ tsp. ginger
¼ tsp. cloves
¼ tsp. mace
¼ tsp. nutmeg

(if you prefer it spicier, just double these 5 spices)

Preheat oven to 350°. To make crust, grind nuts & mix with flour. Cut butter into flour – add water (use a food processor if you have one). Mix well. Roll crust out and place in a 9"x 13" baking dish. Set aside. Blend cream cheese & honey together. Add eggs, pumpkin puree, maple syrup, juice of orange, and spices. Pour into baking dish. Chop apples and distribute evenly over pumpkin filling. Push in gently. Bake at 350° for 1 hour.
Serve plain or topped with freshly made whipped cream!

serves 8

# Creamy Peachberry Pie

<u>Pie Crust</u> (pg. 84)

<u>Fruit Filling</u>:

    1½ cups fresh ripe peaches (peeled & sliced)

    ½ cup blueberries, blackberries, or raspberries

    2 cups plain yogurt

    ⅔ cup maple syrup

    2 eggs

    1 tsp. vanilla

    1 tsp. cinnamon

<u>Crumb Topping</u>:

    ¾ cup whole wheat pastry flour

    4 tbsp. butter

    1½ tbsp. maple syrup

    1 tsp. cinnamon

Make crust as directed — put into a 9" pie plate and flute the edges. Peel peaches and slice into smallish pieces — wash berries and mix peaches and berries in a bowl. In another bowl mix yogurt, maple syrup, vanilla, and cinnamon together — add eggs and beat until blended. Pour the yogurt mixture over fruit and mix well. Set aside while you make the crumb topping.

<u>To make topping</u> .... Melt butter in a small pot — add maple syrup and cinnamon, and then flour. Mix with a fork till crumbly. Pour fruit into pie crust, then sprinkle the crumb topping evenly over the fruit.

Bake at 350° for 50 minutes. Remove from oven and cool to room temperature before serving.

Penny made this one fine day for a picnic...

# Strawberry Rhubarb Sublime

... outrageous topped with vanilla ice cream! The sweetness of the ice cream and the tartness of the fruit is magnificent!

## FRUIT:

- 1 pint fresh strawberries
- 6 lg. stalks of fresh rhubarb
- 1 cup honey
- 2 tsp. cinnamon
- 1/4 tsp. mace
- 1/4 tsp. allspice
- juice of 1 orange (optional)

## CRISPY TOPPING:

- 1 stick butter
- 2 cups whole wheat pastry flour
- 2 cups raw rolled oats
- 1 cup coarsely chopped walnuts
- 1 cup honey

Butter a large 9"x13" baking dish. Wash and cut rhubarb into ¼" pieces. Remove stems from strawberries and wash well. Cut berries in half and put in a good-sized bowl with rhubarb. Add honey, juice of orange, & spices... mix well. Spoon into buttered baking dish. Set aside while you melt butter in a pot on very low heat. Add honey and mix well... then add oats. Mix again, then put in flour and mix with a fork till crumbly. Sprinkle crumbs onto fruit — then sprinkle on nuts. Bake at 350° for 1 hour. Serve warm or at room temperature with a scoop of <u>good</u> vanilla ice cream.

Check at Health Food Stores for ice cream made without sugar. Hagendaaz makes a great honey-vanilla ice cream. You can buy Hagendaaz practically anywhere.

*serves 10 to 12*

# Pumpkin Cream Pie

*...something different for HALLOWEEN, THANKSGIVING... or any occasion!*

Double the recipe for <u>pie crust</u> on pg. 84, or double the recipe for <u>graham Cracker Nut Crust</u> (pg. 81)

- 3 cups pureed pumpkin (I used fresh pumpkin, but canned will suffice)
- 16 oz. cream cheese
- 3 lg. or 4 medium eggs
- 1 cup honey or maple syrup
- 2 to 3 tsp. cinnamon (the more the merrier!)
- 1 tsp. vanilla
- 1 tsp. allspice
- 1 tsp. ginger
- ½ tsp. cloves
- ¼ tsp. mace
- ¼ tsp. nutmeg
- ¼ tsp. orange rind (optional)

Preheat oven to 350°.
Make pie crust as directed. Roll or pat out into a 9"x 13" baking dish. Blend the remaining ingredients together in a mixing bowl, or in a food processor. Pour into crust — and bake at 350° for 1 hour. Remove from oven and let cool to room temperature.
Serve alone... or topped with freshly made whipped cream... pg. 101.

# Pecan Pie

*serve warm... or at room temperature, topped with freshly made whipped cream ... <u>EXQUISITE</u>, yet easy to make*

Whole Wheat Pie Crust (pg. 84)

12 oz. shelled and halved pecans
4 eggs, well beaten
½ stick butter, melted
½ cup barley malt (pg. 107)
½ cup pure maple syrup
1 tbsp. vanilla
1 scant tsp. cinnamon
juice of 1 orange (optional)

Make crust as directed and place in a 9" pie plate. Flute the edges. Place the pecans in crust... set aside. In a medium bowl, beat eggs – add barley malt and maple syrup, vanilla, juice of 1 orange, and cinnamon. Melt the butter and add to egg mixture. Blend well and pour over the pecans in crust.

Bake at 350° for 40 minutes. Remove from oven and let cool.

**DON'T FORGET THE <u>WHIPPED CREAM</u>!**

# Apple Walnut Crunch

serve warm... alone or topped with vanilla ice cream

2/3 cup honey or maple syrup
8 apples
1 cup coarsely chopped walnuts
1 cup raisins
1/2 cup shredded coconut
2 tsp. cinnamon
1/2 tsp. mace
1/4 tsp. cardamom (optional)

CRUMB TOP:

1 stick butter
3/4 cup rolled oats
3/4 cup whole wheat pastry flour

Preheat oven to 350°. Butter a 9"x 13" baking dish. In a small pot, melt butter — add oats & mix well. Add flour and mix with a fork till crumbly. Set aside. Peel, core and slice apples. Put into a bowl & mix with honey, raisins, walnuts, coconut and spices. Mix till apples are well-coated. Spoon apples into buttered dish. Sprinkle crumbs evenly on top of apples.
Bake at 350° for 1 hour.

# Sour Cherry Kuchen

*a lovely pie covered with a perfect custard ... you can use other fruits such as peaches, berries or apples – but pie cherries are such a special treat for us, as they are a rarity in this area*

### CRUST:

- 1 stick butter, room temperature
- 2 cups whole wheat pastry flour
- 3 tbsp. maple syrup or honey

### FRUIT:

- 1½ qts. fresh sour cherries
- 1 cup maple syrup or honey
- 1 tsp. cinnamon

### CUSTARD:

- 1½ cups sour cream or plain yogurt
- 3 eggs, beaten
- 1 tsp. vanilla

Preheat oven to 350°. In a medium bowl, place the flour — cut butter into flour and add honey (a food processor works well for crusts). Then pat dough into bottom of a 9"x 13" baking dish — set aside. Remove pits from cherries. Mix with maple syrup (or honey) and cinnamon. Spoon into crust. In a bowl, beat eggs — add sour cream or yogurt and vanilla... mix well and pour over cherries.
Bake at 350° for 50 minutes. Serve warm or at room temp.

↳ Delicious!

# Nectar-Berry Pie

*... what makes this pie so special is the crust*

Nutty Oat Crust (pg. 82)

12 medium ripe nectarines
½ pint blueberries
½ cup maple syrup
¼ cup apple juice
juice of 1 lemon
3 tbsp. arrowroot

Make crust as directed. Peel and slice nectarines. Wash blueberries.

Take 2 cups of sliced nectarines and put in a smallish pot. Add apple juice, lemon juice, and maple syrup. Bring to a boil. Mix arrowroot into mixture. Turn off heat and stir till thickens, about 5 minutes. Mix _this_ mixture with remaining fruit, and pour into baked pie shell.

This recipe was created by our friend, Ilse, who is a great cook... and is sweet, sweet, sweet! She also knows the true art of note-taking! ♡♡♡♡

# Crumb Top Peach Pie

*— Incredible!!*
*... the best of Sheryl...*

Pie Crust bottom (pg. 84)

5 cups peeled & sliced ripe peaches
2/3 cup honey
1 tbsp. flour
1½ tsp. cinnamon

Crumb Top:

    1 stick butter
    1½ whole wheat pastry flour
    1 tsp. cinnamon

Make crust. Place in 10" pie plate. Peel peaches (if the peaches aren't very ripe, place in boiling water for a minute and the skins will be easy to peel). Slice peaches... mix with honey, 1½ tsp. cinnamon, and 1 tbsp. flour. Mix well, & spoon into pie plate on top of crust. Then, in a small pot, melt butter — add cinnamon & flour — and mix with a fork till crumbly. Sprinkle evenly over peaches.

Bake at 350° for 1 hour, till bubbly and golden.

HELPFUL HINT: place pie on cookie sheet so it won't drip all over the oven.

... don't be afraid to top it off with vanilla ice cream. A little bit can go a long way!

✯ YOU CAN SUBSTITUTE BLUEBERRIES FOR PEACHES ... OR USE ½ PEACHES & ½ BLUEBERRIES

serves 8

# Strawberry Cream Pie

OR... BLUEBERRY CREAM PIE
OR... PEACH CREAM PIE
OR... CREAM CHEESE PIE
...∞

<u>Pie Crust</u> : (pg. 84)

<u>Filling</u> :

- 8 oz. cream cheese
- 2 eggs, beaten
- 1 cup sour cream
- 2/3 cup pure maple syrup
- 1 tsp. vanilla

<u>Fruit</u> :

- 1 pint strawberries (or blueberries... or any other berries... or combination of berries. Peaches are good, too. Use your imagination!)
- 1/3 cup maple syrup
- pinch of cinnamon

Make crust. Blend all the <u>filling</u> ingredients and pour into crust. Bake at 350° for 40 minutes.

Remove from oven and let cool thoroughly. Refrigerate. Wash and remove stems from berries. Mix with $\frac{1}{3}$ cup maple syrup, and cinnamon.

When serving pie, top with fresh berries.

You can add freshly whipped cream, too ... if you're <u>mad</u> enough.

*serves 6 to 8*

# Peach Cobbler

12 medium-ripe peaches
      (peeled and quartered)
½ cup honey
juice of ½ lemon
1 tsp. cinnamon
1⅔ cup whole wheat pastry flour
⅓ cup finely ground walnuts
4 tbsp. butter
1 tbsp. baking powder
1 egg, beaten
⅔ cup milk
1 tsp. vanilla

Preheat oven to 350° — butter a 9"x13" baking dish. Place the peaches in a large pot and cover with water. Put a lid on pot and bring to a boil. As soon as water comes to a boil, pour into sink and run cold water on peaches. When they are cool enough to handle, peel them... remove pits and cut into quarters. Place peaches back in pot — mix with honey, lemon juice and cinnamon. Then pour into baking dish... set aside. In a bowl, mix flour & baking powder together. Cut in the butter till flour looks mealy. Beat egg, milk, and vanilla together and mix with flour. Drop batter by tablespoonful evenly over peaches. Then place in oven & bake 30 min. or till top is firm and golden.

Serve warm or at room temperature topped with a good vanilla ice cream or whipped cream.

*serves 8*

# Divine Apple Cream Torte

*— one of our favorites... try it!
Can't say enough about it — really is DIVINE!*

Pastry — for one pie crust (pg. 84)

5 or 6 lg. apples — peeled, cored & sliced

8 oz. cream cheese

2/3 cup maple syrup or honey

1 tsp. vanilla

1 egg, beaten

1 tsp. cinnamon

1/4 tsp. mace or nutmeg (optional)

1/2 cup coarsely chopped walnuts

2 tbsp. maple syrup or honey

Make crust as directed. Place in pie plate and flute edges... set aside. In a large bowl – beat cream cheese, egg, $\frac{1}{3}$ cup maple syrup or honey, and vanilla together. Pour cream mixture into pie crust. Peel and slice apples – mix with $\frac{1}{3}$ cup maple syrup or honey, cinnamon, and mace. Spread apples evenly over cream mixture. Mix chopped walnuts with 2 tablespoons maple syrup or honey, and sprinkle evenly over apples.

Bake at 350° for 50 minutes.
Cool to room temperature and serve.

*serves 8*

# Honey Glazed Blueberry Tart

an incredible summer pie... the berries are basically uncooked & glazed. It is just as good with fresh strawberries. <u>Must</u> be topped with freshly whipped cream — for the full effect!

(...I can't tell you how wonderful this recipe is... <u>try it</u>!)

Crust - pg. 84

2 full pints of fresh blueberries (or strawberries — <u>or</u> try mixing half of each)

⅔ cup boiling water

1 cup honey or maple syrup

3 tbsp. arrowroot (pg.

1 tsp. cinnamon

a pinch of mace... if you like


Preheat oven to 350°. Make crust as directed. Put into a 9" pie plate — prick holes in bottom of crust with a fork. Bake at 350° for 15 minutes or till golden. Remove from heat and cool.

While crust is baking, wash your berries & remove stems. Mash about ⅓ of them (try to get the ripest ones) with a potato masher or whatever other utensil you like to use for _mashing_. Place the remaining whole berries in a good-sized bowl and set aside. In a smallish pot – place mashed berries, boiling water, honey, arrowroot, cinnamon, and mace. Place pot on low heat & simmer till it thickens somewhat, stirring constantly..... takes about 5 minutes. You don't want it to get _too_ thick. Remove from heat and let cool 5 min. Then mix with the whole berries till they (the whole berries) are coated well. Spoon into baked crust. Cool ½ hour, then refrigerate several hours.

Serve chilled with a meager _or_ generous helping of freshly made whipped cream.

↳ truly amazing!

serves 8

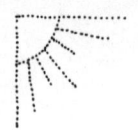

# Mango Mania

— an unusual mango cream pie

<u>Graham Cracker Nut Crust</u> (for 9" pie plate)

- 1 cup graham crackers (whole wheat — pg. 105)
- ½ cup chopped almonds
- ¼ cup butter or soy margarine (pg. 103)
- 1 tbsp. honey

Blend graham crackers and almonds in a food processor, blender, or by hand till finely crushed. In a small pot, melt butter — add honey, nuts and graham cracker crumbs. Mix well and then press into pie plate with fingers, covering bottom evenly and up the sides. Take a fork and make holes in crust. Then bake at 350° for 7 minutes. Remove from oven, and set aside to cool.

## Filling

- 8 oz. cream cheese
- 1 cup plain yogurt
- ¼ cup powdered milk (optional)
- ½ cup honey
- 1 tsp. vanilla
- 4 very ripe mangoes (save 2 for top of pie... remove skins & pits)
- ¼ cup shredded coconut

Sprinkle coconut on baked crust. In a food processor, blender or mixer – blend all the filling ingredients (using only 2 mangoes). Pour into shell and freeze for 2 hrs. or till solid. Before serving, remove from freezer and let sit till slightly softened (about ½ hour). Slice 2 remaining mangoes and place on top of pie...
... and enjoy!

This pie was conceived by our creative friend, Caroline, who, needing to use up some very ripe mangoes, came up with this palatable delight! ♡♡

*serves 8*

# Crumble Berry Pie

*extraordinary!*

<u>CRUMB CRUST</u>:

- 1½ cups whole wheat pastry flour
- 1 stick butter
- 3 tbsp. maple syrup or honey

<u>FRUIT</u>:

- 1 pint fresh blueberries
- 1 pint sour cream (2 cups)
- 2 eggs, beaten
- ⅔ cup maple syrup or honey
- 1 tsp. vanilla
- 1 tsp. cinnamon
- ¼ tsp. mace (optional)

<u>Crust</u> – Melt butter in a small pot. Add 3 tbsp. maple syrup or honey, and mix well – then add flour. Mix with a fork till crumbly. Pat ½ of crumbs into 9" pie plate & save ½ for top of pie.

In a medium sized bowl, simply combine all the <u>fruit</u> ingredients. Mix well. Spoon into crust. Sprinkle evenly with remaining crumbs and bake at 350° for 50 minutes. Remove from oven and cool to room temperature before serving.

WONDERFUL!

*serves 6 to 8*

# Black Raspberry Crisp

*black raspberries are available for a short time...*
*... and they're such a special treat*
⤷ *simple, yet divine!*

2 pints fresh black raspberries
1 stick butter
2 cups whole wheat pastry flour
$\frac{2}{3}$ cup honey or maple syrup
1 tsp. cinnamon
1 tsp. vanilla
$\frac{1}{4}$ tsp. mace (optional)

Preheat oven to 350°. Butter a 9"x 13" baking dish. Wash berries... put into bowl and mix with honey and spices. Spoon into baking dish. In a small pot, melt butter ⁓ add vanilla, and mix. Add flour and mix with a fork till crumbly. Sprinkle evenly over berries and bake 40 minutes at 350°. Serve warm or at room temperature, topped with a serious serving of vanilla ice cream.

serves 8

# Punk-in Pie

<u>CRUST</u> — use Graham Cracker Nut Crust, <u>doubled</u>, on pg. 81, or double the crust recipe on pg. 84.

<u>FILLING</u> —

- 2 cups pureed pumpkin
- 2 cups sour cream or yogurt
- 3 eggs, beaten
- 1 cup honey
- 2 tbsp. cinnamon
- 1/2 tsp. allspice
- 1/2 tsp. ginger
- 1/4 tsp. mace
- 1/4 tsp. cardamom
- 1/4 tsp. cloves
- 1 tsp. vanilla

Make crust as directed — put into a 9"x 13" baking dish. Then, simply mix all the filling ingredients together. Pour into baking dish. Bake at 350° for 1 hour. Serve at room temperature... alone, or with ...... you got it .... <u>WHIPPED CREAM</u>!!

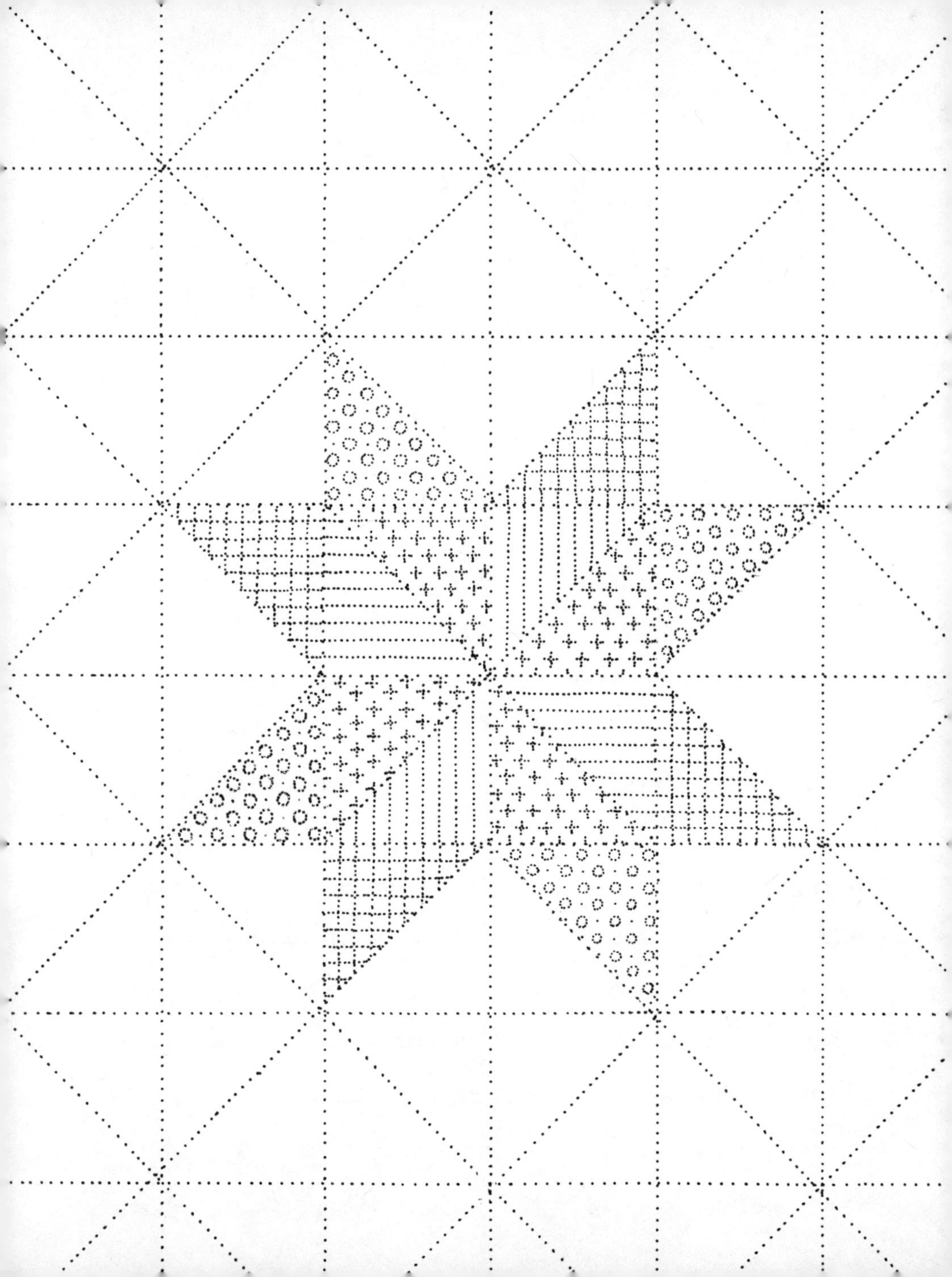

# Cakes, Cookies, Brownies, etc.

Carrot Cake .................................................. 36
Spicey Pear Cake ......................................... 38
Carob Fudge Brownies ................................ 40
Baklava ........................................................ 42
Old-Fashioned Peach/Pear Shortcake ...... 44
Pumpkin Cake ............................................. 46
Date-Nut Chip Brownies ............................ 48
Poppy Seed Strudel .................................... 50
Pineapple Cheesecake ................................ 52
Simple Spice Cake ....................................... 54
Honey Dews ................................................ 56
Apple Walnut Cake ..................................... 58
Schnecken ................................................... 60
Blustery Day Oatmeal Cookies .................. 62

serves 8 to 10

## Carrot Cake

...thanks to (Herbert) Birdsfoot

2 cups whole wheat pastry flour
1 tsp. baking soda
1 tsp. baking powder
1 tsp. cinnamon
1 tsp. ginger
1/4 tsp. mace
1/4 tsp. nutmeg
3 cups grated raw carrot
1 cup safflower oil
1 cup honey
1 cup raisins
1½ cups chopped walnuts
4 eggs, beaten

Preheat oven to 350°. Butter a 9"x 13" baking dish. In a large bowl — mix oil, honey, and beaten eggs together; and grated carrot, raisins, & walnuts. Mix well. Mix dry ingredients together and slowly add to liquid ingredients, making sure to incorporate well. Spoon into buttered dish and bake 1 hour, or till cake tester comes out clean. Cool. When completely cooled, frost with cream cheese icing. (pg. 100)

Herbert Birdsfoot is a "guy" from Sesame Street... but he _really_ lives in Bucks County, PA. ♡

# Spicey Pear Cake

*a lovely, yet simple cake created by our friend, Denise... who is one of the world's finest cooks!*

- 1 cup butter, softened
- ½ cup maple syrup granules (pg. 106)
- ¼ cup molasses
- ¼ cup maple syrup
- 1 egg
- 1½ cups whole wheat pastry flour
- ¾ tsp. sea salt
- ¾ tsp. baking soda
- ¼ tsp. ginger
- ½ tsp. cinnamon
- ¼ tsp. mace (optional)
- ½ cup boiled water
- 2 lg. red or yellow Bartlett pears

Preheat oven to 350°. Butter an 8"x 8" cake pan. Wash pears — remove cores, then cut into thin slices and place evenly over bottom of cake pan... set aside. In a large bowl — cream butter, the 3 sweeteners, and 1 egg together well. In another bowl, sift dry ingredients together — begin adding to the butter mixture, alternating with the boiled water. Beat till well blended. Spoon batter evenly over pears in cake pan, then bake at 350° for 35 to 40 minutes.

Serve warm or at room temperature.

serves 10 to 12

## Carob Fudge Brownies

good plain... but <u>divine</u> topped with vanilla ice cream or freshly made whipped cream... or a little of each! There <u>are</u> occasions for madness — enjoy it!!

1 stick butter
1 cup whole wheat pastry flour
1 cup honey
6 oz. carob chips or pieces
2 eggs, beaten
1 cup coarsely chopped walnuts
1 tsp. vanilla


Butter a 9"x 13" baking dish. Preheat oven to

350°. Melt carob and butter together on a low heat or in a double boiler. When melted, scrape into a "large-ish" bowl. Add honey, beaten eggs, and vanilla. Mix well — then add flour. Mix well. Then add chopped nuts, and mix well *again*!

Spoon into buttered baking dish... and bake ½ hour, or till center is set.

Cool and cut into squares.

This recipe is a combination of mine and that of a lovely woman, named Jackie, from Virginia, who crossed my path one fine day.

serves 6 to 8

# Baklava

*a Greek dessert pastry made with honey and nuts ⁓ goo·ey & wonderful!*

- ½ box of filo dough (pg. 104)
- 1 cup chopped almonds
- 1 cup chopped walnuts
- 1 stick butter
- 1 cup honey
- 2 tsp. cinnamon
- ¼ tsp. mace
- ¼ tsp. cloves
- juice of 1 lemon

Melt butter in a smallish saucepan and mix in honey, lemon juice, & spices. Chop nuts and mix together in a bowl. In a buttered baking dish, place 3 sheets of filo flat — sprinkle with $\frac{1}{3}$ of nuts & drizzle $\frac{1}{3}$ of butter/honey mixture on top of nuts. Repeat 2 more times with sheets of filo and $\frac{1}{3}$'s of nuts and butter mixture... end with filo on top of nuts, and drizzle liquid on top. Bake at 325° for 35 to 40 minutes, or till golden. Cut into squares and serve warm... or at room temperature.

*serves 6 to 8*

# Old Fashioned Peach/Pear Shortcake

4 cups fresh peaches, peeled & sliced
2 cups fresh pears
½ cup maple syrup or honey
1 tsp. cinnamon

### SHORTCAKE

2 cups whole wheat pastry flour
2 tbsp. maple syrup or honey
3 tsp. baking powder
4 tbsp. butter
⅔ cup raw milk (pg. 105)
1 cup heavy cream for whipping (pg. 101)

Peel and slice peaches and pears — place in a bowl and mix with ½ c. maple syrup or honey — refrigerate. Preheat oven to 350°. Butter a 9" round cake pan. Mix flour & baking powder together in a bowl... add 2 tbsp. maple syrup or honey — blend, then cut in butter until mixture looks mealy. Mix in milk thoroughly. Place dough on a floured surface & knead a minute or two. Pat the dough into the buttered pan and bake 20 min. or till golden in color. Remove shortcake from pan & cut into 2 layers (cut the cake horizontally... put one layer on a plate, cut side up & spoon half of fruit on top. Top with other layer — spoon remaining fruit on top... and top it all off with freshly whipped cream.

YOU CAN USE BERRIES WITH THE PEACHES... OR BERRIES ALONE... OR ANY COMBINATION THAT PLEASES YOU.

# Pumpkin Cake

*a hearty, moist cake — serve alone or frost with cream cheese icing*

- 3 cups whole wheat pastry flour
- 1 cup honey or maple syrup
- 1 cup safflower oil
- 2 cups pureed pumpkin
- 4 eggs
- 3 tsp. baking powder
- 1 tsp. baking soda
- 1 tsp. vanilla
- ½ cup chopped walnuts
- ½ cup raisins
- 2 tsp. cinnamon
- ½ tsp. nutmeg
- ½ tsp. mace
- ½ tsp. ginger
- ½ tsp. cloves

Preheat oven to 350°. Butter a 9"x13" cake pan. In a large bowl – mix honey, oil, and pumpkin. Beat till well blended. Start adding eggs one at a time, beating after each egg is added. Mix dry ingredients together and begin adding to liquid mixture, blending well. Add raisins and nuts. Pour into buttered pan & bake 40 to 50 min., or till tester comes out clean. Remove from oven and let cool to room temperature. Serve as is, or frosted with cream cheese icing (pg. 100).

Try growing or buying Hubbard squash or pie pumpkins. Peel and steam, then puree. It's alot less expensive than buying canned pumpkin. It freezes well – or can be "put up" (as in _home_ canning). It's ecological, too!

makes about 24 large brownies

# Date Nut Chip Brownies

*a winner!! — and very simple to make
... given to us by our pal, Jude*

    1 cup chopped pitted dates
    1½ cups boiling water
    1½ tsp. baking soda
    1½ sticks butter, softened
    ⅔ cup honey
    2 eggs
    1¾ cups whole wheat pastry flour
    ¾ tsp. baking soda
    ½ tsp. baking powder
    1 cup chopped walnuts
    10 oz. carob chips

Preheat oven to 350°. Butter a 9"x13" cake pan. Combine first three ingredients — let stand ½ hr. till cooled. Meanwhile, cream butter and honey together. Add eggs, and beat till light and fluffy. Mix in the cooled date mixture and blend well. Mix dry ingredients together and add to batter. Mix till well blended, but do not overbeat. Stir in chopped nuts and carob chips. Pour into cake pan and bake at 350° for 45 to 55 minutes, or till cake tester comes out clean. Remove from oven and cool completely before cutting into brownie squares.

They're actually _best_ baked the day before serving, if possible ... if it's not possible, they're still great!

# Poppy Seed Strudel

*a wondrous light pastry filled with poppy seeds, raisins and prune butter*

<u>DOUGH</u> (prepare early in the day & allow to chill a few hours before using)

- ½ lb. softened butter
- 1 cup sour cream
- 1 egg yolk
- 3 cups flour

<u>ROLLING-OUT INGREDIENTS</u>

- ¾ cup whole wheat pastry flour
- 2 tsp. (good-sized) cinnamon

<u>FILLING</u>

- 1½ cups raisins
- 1½ cups poppy seeds
- 2 cups prune butter (ask for at Health Food Stores... also sold in supermarkets, under the name, LEKVAR)

Dough — Cream softened butter, egg yolk & sour cream in a large bowl... gradually add flour till smooth. Divide into 4 balls — roll each ball in a little flour, then place in a plastic bag. Refrigerate a few hours. When ready to begin again, mix all the filling ingredients in a bowl — set aside. In another bowl, mix the "rolling-out ingredients" together — dust a wooden board with some of it, then take the dough from the refrigerator and roll one of the balls out until it is thin, thin, thin. Spread $\frac{1}{4}$ of the filling ingredients evenly over the dough, then roll the dough up like a jelly roll & place onto a buttered cookie sheet. Repeat the process with remaining dough and filling. Place the strudels side-by-side on the cookie sheet, then bake in a 350° oven for 45 minutes. Remove from oven and let cool for $\frac{1}{2}$ hour. Then slice into 3 or 4" slices and serve.

BREW A POT OF HERB TEA ... AND ENJOY !

*serves 10 to 12*

# Pineapple Cheesecake

*a light and delicious cheesecake —*
*...easy to make and goes a long way*

<u>CRUST</u> – use <u>Pie Crust</u> on pg. 84, or <u>Graham Cracker Nut Crust</u> on pg. 81 ... but make sure you <u>double</u> either recipe

<u>FRUIT</u> –   16 oz. can crushed pineapple

2 tbsp. arrowroot (pg. 103) or cornstarch

3 tbsp. honey or maple syrup

<u>CHEESE FILLING</u> –

16 oz. cream cheese

½ cup honey or maple syrup

2 tbsp. flour

1 tbsp. vanilla

juice of 1 lemon

4 eggs

3 cups milk

cinnamon for top

Preheat oven to 325°. Make crust as directed and roll out to fit a 9"x 13" baking dish. Set aside. In a smallish pot, mix pineapple (juice and all), arrowroot or cornstarch, and honey together — simmer on a low heat for 5 minutes or so, till it thickens. Spoon evenly over pie crust. Cream the cream cheese, honey, flour, vanilla, and lemon juice together. Add eggs and milk, and beat until well blended. Then pour over fruit in baking dish. Sprinkle with cinnamon and bake at 325° for 1 hour 10 minutes. Remove from oven and let cool to room temperature — then refrigerate a few hours before serving.

... *Divine* — and truly luscious! You could use blueberries or strawberries instead of, or with the pineapple. Just mash up your berries and improvise.

This dessert is *almost* as wonderful as our friend, Sheryl, who created it. ♡ ♡ ♡

*serves 10 to 12*

# Simple Spice Cake

*very wholesome ... and tasty*

2½ cups whole wheat pastry flour
1 cup maple syrup or honey
1 stick butter
1 cup yogurt
1 cup raisins
2 eggs
3 tsp. baking powder
3 tsp. cinnamon
1 tsp. nutmeg
½ tsp. cloves
½ tsp. allspice
½ tsp. cardamom
½ tsp. mace
½ tsp. ginger

Preheat oven to 350°. Butter a 9"x13" baking pan. Cream maple syrup and butter together. Add eggs — beat till light and fluffy. Mix the spices and baking powder with the flour... begin adding to butter mixture, alternating with yogurt. Blend well. Add raisins and mix well. Pour into buttered baking pan.

Bake at 350° for 40 to 45 minutes or till tester comes out clean. Remove and let cool. Can be served warm with butter or cream cheese... or you can make an orange cream cheese icing (pg. 100).

Ice when cooled to room temperature. Cut into squares and serve.

# Honey Dews

*a crispy fried pastry dripping with honey — serve with fresh fruit and a cup of tea ... perfect!*

THANKS TRACEY

1½ to 2 cups whole wheat pastry flour

3 eggs beaten slightly

½ tsp. sea salt (optional)

honey

peanut oil – for frying


Mix flour and salt together in a small bowl. Make a well in the flour & pour the beaten eggs into the well. Blend with a wooden spoon to make a soft dough — then turn onto a floured surface and knead in enough flour to make a dough that can easily be rolled into thin sheets. Before rolling, divide dough into 2 or 3 parts (for easy rolling). Roll out and then cut sheets into strips ($\frac{1}{2}$" x $\frac{1}{4}$") and then deep fry in <u>hot</u> oil (use a skillet and put in a few inches of oil — flip them if you have to, so they fry evenly). Drain thoroughly by placing the dews on paper towels, then put on plate and drizzle with honey. Then place more honey dews on top and drizzle them... and so on. You'll have a good-sized stack — pull them apart and start munching!

*serves 8*

## **Apple Walnut Cake**

*this wonderful cake can be mixed in a large bowl with a wooden spoon. It's an old-fashioned recipe... from the days before the electric mixer.*

    4 to 6 med./lg. apples (about 3 cups)
    1 cup chopped walnuts
    ¼ cup honey
    1 ~~tbsp.~~ cinnamon
    ¼ tsp. mace

Peel, core and slice apples. Put in a bowl — chop walnuts and add to apples, along with honey, cinnamon and mace. Mix well and set aside.

<u>*Batter*</u>:

    3½ cups whole wheat pastry flour

    4 tsp. baking powder (I know it's alot, but it's o.k. — just use aluminum-free baking powder... pg. 103)

    1 cup honey

    1 cup safflower oil

    1 cup orange juice

    4 eggs

    1 tsp. vanilla

Preheat oven to 350°. Put all batter ingredients into one bowl — and b<u>ea</u>t, b<u>ea</u>t, b<u>ea</u>t with a wooden spoon till well blended. Butter and flour a tube cake pan. Spoon ½ of batter into prepared pan. Place ½ of apples evenly over the batter — then spread rest of batter evenly over apples, then rest of apples evenly over batter! Push the apples on top gently into the batter with the wooden spoon. Bake at 350° for 1 hour or 1 hr. 10 min., or till cake tester comes out clean.

Remove from oven and cool completely.

# Schnecken

*a very old family recipe... an incredible light pastry filled with raisins, nuts, etc. Takes some time to prepare, but well worth the effort!*

— *a good rainy... or snowy day project*

## PASTRY DOUGH

- 3 cups whole wheat pastry flour
- ½ lb. butter, softened (2 sticks)
- 1 cup sour cream
- 1 egg yolk

## ROLLING-OUT INGREDIENTS

- ½ cup flour
- 2 tsp. cinnamon

## FILLING

- 1 cup chopped walnuts
- 1 cup raisins
- 1 cup strawberry jam (made w/ honey - ask for at Health Food Store)
- ½ cup grated coconut
- ¼ cup honey

<u>Dough</u> — Cream softened butter, egg yolk and sour cream together. Gradually add flour till you form a smooth ball. Divide into 4 separate balls and roll each ball in some flour. Put balls in a plastic bag and refrigerate several hours or overnight.

When ready to <u>roll</u>, combine all the filling ingredients together in a bowl, and mix well. In another small bowl or cup, combine "rolling-out ingredients" and dust a wooden surface with some of it. Roll one ball at a time out on the floured surface, into very thin circles. Cut circle into 8 triangular wedges △. Place a tbsp. of filling at wide end and roll up like a crescent. Place each schnecken on a lightly buttered cookie sheet. Bake at 350° for 20 to 30 min., or till golden brown. Remove from oven & cool to room temperature before serving.

<u>WATCH OUT</u>! ... THEY'RE ADDICTIVE!!

# Blustery Day Oatmeal Cookies

*...it was snowing and blowing the day these were conceived and WINNIE THE POOH was on my mind........*

3 cups raw oats
1½ sticks butter
1 cup whole wheat pastry flour
1 cup maple syrup or honey
1 cup raisins
½ cup coarsely chopped walnuts
1 egg, beaten
2 tbsp. water
2 tsp. cinnamon
1 tsp. vanilla
1 tsp. baking soda

Preheat oven to 350°. Butter 2 cookie sheets. Cream butter, honey, egg, water, and vanilla until light and fluffy. Mix dry ingredients together, including oats. Add to butter mixture a little at a time, incorporating well. Add spices, raisins, and walnuts. Mix well. Spoon or drop cookies by tablespoonful onto cookie sheet. Bake at 350° for approximately 15 minutes or until edges are brownish.

> The more it snows...
>     (Tiddely Pom)
> The more it goes...
>     (Tiddely Pom)
> The more it goes...
>     (Tiddely Pom)
> ...on snowing.
> And nobody knows...
>     (Tiddely Pom)
> How cold my toes...
>     (Tiddely Pom)
> How cold my toes...
>     (Tiddely Pom)
> ...are growing.

A.A. Milne
"House at Pooh Corner."

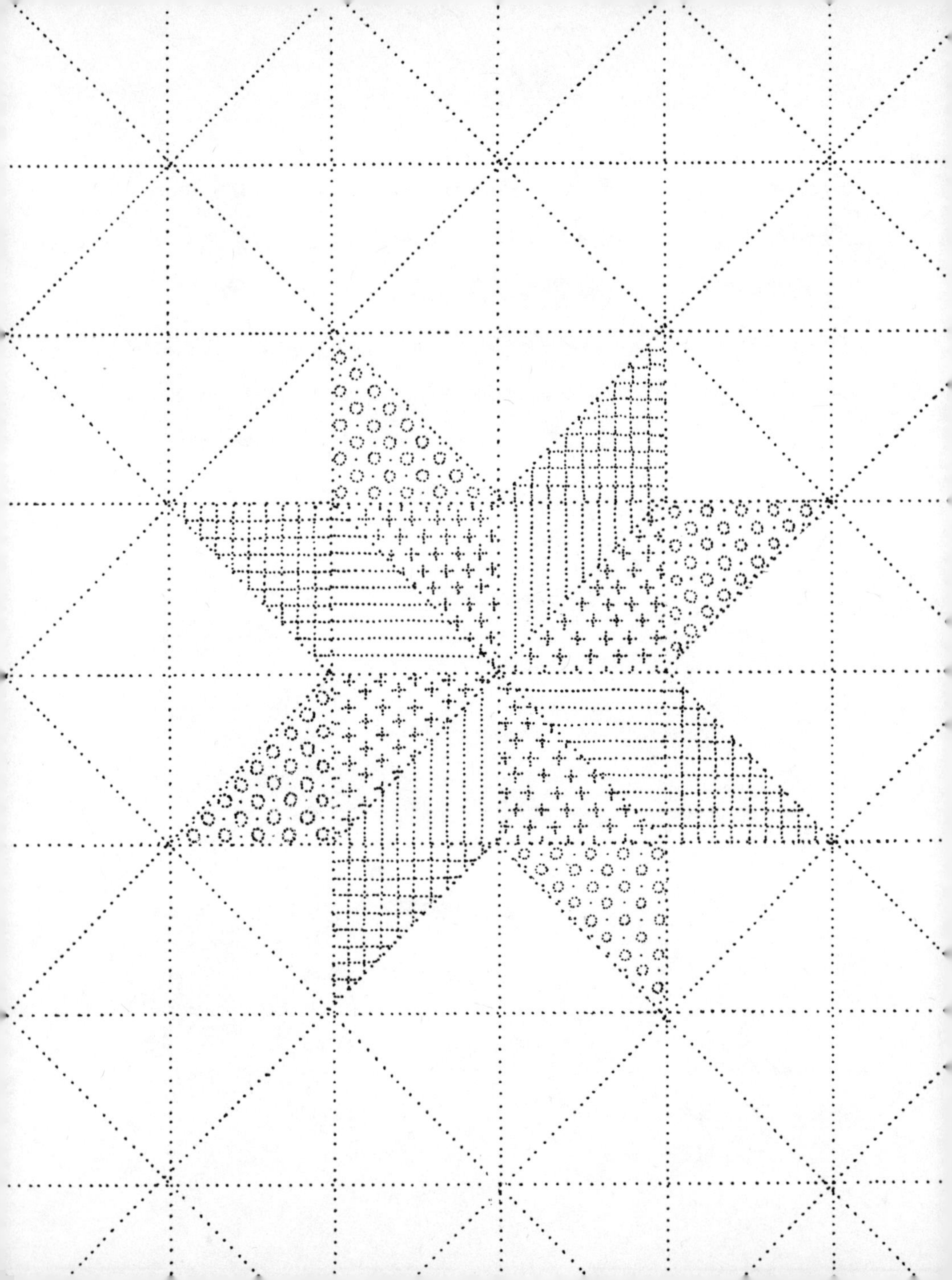

# Muffins, Crusts, Fritters, etc.

Banana Chip Muffins ................................ 66
Cranberry Nut Muffins ............................. 68
Date-Nut Muffins ..................................... 70
Gingerbread Muffins ................................ 72
Golden Corn Fritters ............................... 74
Banana Nut Muffins ................................. 76
Whole Wheat Cinnamon Buns ................. 78
Graham Cracker Nut Crust ..................... 81
Nutty Oat Crust ....................................... 82
Wonderfully Whole Wheaty Pie Crust ........ 84

# Banana Chip Muffins

1½ cups whole wheat pastry flour
⅓ cup melted butter
3 pureed bananas
½ cup chopped walnuts
6 oz. carob chips
½ cup shredded coconut
½ cup maple syrup granules (pg. 106)
   or ½ c. maple syrup or ½ c. honey
½ tsp. baking soda
½ tsp. sea salt (optional)
1 tsp. baking powder
2 eggs, beaten

Preheat oven to 375°. Butter a 12-muffin tin. Mix dry ingredients together in a bowl. Melt butter & add to flour. Beat eggs and add. Puree bananas — mix with maple syrup granules and add to flour. Mix well. Then add coconut, carob chips and chopped walnuts. Blend well. Then spoon into muffin tin(s).

Bake at 375° for 30 minutes.

# Cranberry Nut Muffins

~ a lovely holiday tea muffin ... wonderful served with an orange butter

- 2 cups whole wheat pastry flour
- ½ cup honey or maple syrup
- ½ cup orange juice
- 2 eggs, beaten
- 3 tbsp. butter, melted
- 1½ cups <u>fresh</u> cranberries
- 2 tsp. baking powder
- ½ cup chopped walnuts
- 1 tbsp. grated orange rind (optional)

Preheat oven to 350°. Butter a 12-muffin tin. Mix flour and baking powder together. In a bowl, blend honey, orange juice, beaten eggs, and melted butter with flour mixture. Add cranberries, walnuts and orange rind. Mix thoroughly, but do not overmix. Spoon into buttered muffin tin(s), and bake 30 minutes — or till cake tester comes out clean. Remove from oven and let cool thoroughly.

Serve with butter — to which you can add a little honey or maple syrup... a little orange juice...

## Date Nut Muffins

serve with tea — with honey, butter or honey-ed cream cheese

2 cups whole wheat pastry flour
5 tbsp. butter
½ cup maple syrup or honey
½ cup boiling water
1 cup pitted dates, chopped
1 egg, beaten
2½ tsp. baking powder
½ cup chopped walnuts
1 tsp. vanilla
1 tsp. cinnamon

Preheat oven to 350°. Butter a 12-muffin tin. Put dates in a bowl & pour boiling water on top. Add maple syrup or honey. Stir well — set aside. Mix flour & baking powder together. Beat egg, & add beaten egg and vanilla to date mixture. Add flour mixture — beat really well. Add walnuts & cinnamon. Spoon into 12-muffin tin(s). Bake at 350° for 30 minutes ... or till cake tester comes out clean. Cool. Serve alone, with butter, or with cream cheese.

You can add a little maple syrup or honey to butter or cream cheese, and beat. You can also squeeze in an orange or a lemon for a nice touch.

makes 24

# Gingerbread Muffins

... *light and lovely!*

given to us by *Dianne* ... the *true* muffin lady

2½ cups whole wheat pastry flour
1½ tsp. baking soda
1 tsp. cinnamon
1 tsp. ginger
1 tbsp. grated orange rind (optional)
2 eggs, beaten
½ cup light molasses
½ cup honey
1 cup hot water
½ cup butter
1 cup finely chopped pecans

Preheat oven to 375°. In a smallish pot, melt butter — then pour into a large bowl (use a spatula to get all the butter out of the pot). Mix dry ingredients together in another bowl. Then, in third bowl, mix the liquid ingredients together. Start adding the dry and the liquid alternately to the butter. Mix until well blended, then add the chopped nuts. Mix again. Spoon into muffin shells... (about ⅓ full) Bake at 375° for 20 minutes.

You could top with a little cream cheese icing (pg.    )... but they are _perfect_ alone.

## Golden Corn Fritters

...makes a lovely breakfast or dessert...
with a fruit salad and a spot of tea!

½ cup whole wheat pastry flour
½ cup corn meal
2 tbsp. maple syrup or honey
1 egg, beaten
½ cup corn kernels (fresh preferred!)
¼ cup milk
½ tsp. baking powder (pg. 103)

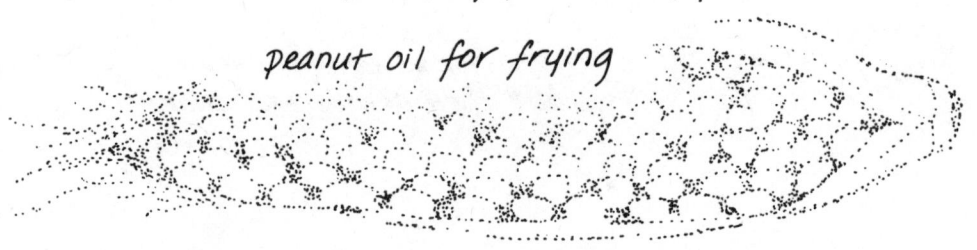

peanut oil for frying

In a good-sized bowl, mix flour, corn meal, and baking powder together. In another bowl, beat egg, honey or maple syrup, and milk together. Add corn kernels. Pour into dry mixture and blend well. Pour about 5 tbsp. oil into a skillet and heat slowly till real hot. Drop batter by tablespoonfuls into skillet and fry fritters till golden brown... turning only once. Cook about 2 minutes on each side. Drain on paper towels and serve immediately — with or without maple syrup. Slice some fresh peaches or berries on top, and, if you'd like, top with whipped cream or vanilla ice cream.

... why not ........ take it as far as it goes!

*makes 12 muffins*

## Nutty Banana Muffins

*a simple tea muffin — serve with butter and a good honey jam ... or simply alone*

- 2 cups whole wheat pastry flour
- 1 stick butter
- ½ cup maple syrup or honey
- 2 eggs
- 3 large ripe mashed bananas
- 1 tsp. baking soda
- 1 tsp. baking powder
- 1 tsp. vanilla
- ½ cup chopped walnuts
- 1 tsp. cinnamon
- ½ tsp. mace
- ½ tsp. nutmeg
- ½ tsp. cardamom

Preheat oven to 350°. Butter a 12-muffin tin. Cream butter & maple syrup (or honey) until light and fluffy. Add eggs and beat well. Mix dry ingredients together, and add to butter mixture. Mash bananas & mix walnuts, vanilla and spices in with banana. Fold banana mixture into batter, then spoon into muffin tin(s).

Bake 30 minutes or until cake tester comes out clean. Remove from heat and cool. Serve warm or at room temperature, with butter and a nice honey fruit jam.

# Deliciously Wholesome Whole Wheat Cinnamon Buns

makes about 2 dozen ... a <u>great</u> dessert!
— Also a wonderful Sunday breakfast treat.

### <u>BUNS</u>:

- 6 cups whole wheat flour
   (not whole wheat pastry flour... see pg. 104)
- 2 cups warm milk
- 2 tbsp. baking yeast
- ¼ cup warm water
- 1 tbsp. sea salt (optional)
- 3 tbsp. oil
- ½ cup honey
- ½ cup wheat germ (optional)

### <u>TOPPING</u>:

- 1 stick butter
- 1 cup honey
- 1 tbsp. cinnamon
- 1 cup raisins
- 1 cup chopped walnuts

In a small bowl, dissolve yeast in warm water and add 2 tbsp. honey — set aside. Heat milk. In a large bowl, combine salt, oil, and warm milk. Add rest of honey and blend well... add wheat germ. Begin adding flour a cup at a time until a runny dough is formed — add the softened yeast mixture. Stir well and continue adding flour until dough comes away from the sides of bowl. Turn dough out on a floured board and knead for 8 minutes, adding flour until dough is no longer sticky. Place dough in an oiled bowl...(spin around and flip over, so top gets oiled, too). Cover with a towel and set in a warm place to rise. When dough has doubled in bulk, punch down and knead again for

a few minutes. Separate into 2 balls — roll each ball out flat. In a small pot, melt butter — add honey and cinnamon... mix. Brush some of butter/honey mixture on top of dough — then sprinkle on half of the chopped nuts and raisins. Roll dough up like a jellyroll and slice in $\frac{3}{4}$" slices. Place, touching each other, in an oiled cake pan — and brush generously again with butter/honey mixture. Repeat with 2nd ball of dough. Let rise 15 minutes, while oven is pre-heating to 350°.
Bake for 40 to 45 minutes. Serve warm with lots of butter!

This comes from our pal, Lizzy — down in old West Virginia.

# Graham Cracker Nut Crust

½ cup crushed whole wheat graham crackers (pg. 81)
½ cup whole wheat pastry flour
1 cup finely chopped walnuts or almonds (or combination of both)
6 tbsp. butter
2 tbsp. honey or maple syrup


Melt butter on a low heat in a medium pot; add honey and mix well. Mix flour, crushed graham crackers and chopped nuts together. Gradually add to butter and honey mixture, mixing with a fork till crumbly. Press into a 9" pie plate.

# Nutty Oat Crust

use this crust recipe for apple pies — or for any fruit pie ..... it is very unusual and delicious
— thanks Ilse

1 cup roasted almonds
¾ cup rolled oats
½ cup shredded coconut
¾ cup whole wheat pastry flour
nice dash of cinnamon
smaller dash of mace
½ cup maple syrup
½ cup safflower oil

In a food processor or blender, process almonds and oats together to make a fine meal. Mix with remaining dry ingredients — put in a bowl. In another bowl, blend maple syrup and safflower oil together well and then add to dry ingredients. Mix well. Butter a deep dish 9" to 10" pie plate. Pat the dough into the dish, bringing the dough up on the sides (makes a thick crust). Bake at 350° for 10 min., till lightly browned. Do not overbake. If the pastry puffs up while baking, just press it down with your fingers.

# Wonderfully Whole Wheaty Pie Crust

1 cup whole wheat pastry flour
6 tbsp. butter
2 to 3 tbsp. cold water

If you have a food processor, use it! If not, simply cut the butter into the flour in a bowl. When butter and flour are mealy-looking, add water a little at a time, enough to form dough into a ball. Roll out on floured board, or between 2 pieces of waxed paper. Place in a 9" or 10" pie plate, and flute edges.

This crust is really very delicious. The whole wheat pastry flour is complimented by the butter — created an extremely flavorful and light pastry.

Most of us go through the daily trauma
Of what to cook for dinner,
And what a divine feeling,
When we come through with a winner.

So we eat, and then we eat some more,
Ah, nothing gives us greater pleasure,
But the real treat is yet to come
A dessert that everyone will treasure.

Now we all have our failures
When creating a masterpiece,
Such as, "Oh no, I ran out of eggs,"
Or, "Oops, too much yeast!"

So we perservere and we try again
till finally it turns out right,
And lo and behold we end up with
A natural foods delight!

All of those fine ingredients,
So good for the body and soul,
But beware, if you eat too much,
One could buldge with an extra roll!

We're proud to share our ideas with you.
So enjoy, and bake to your heart's delight;
With some written guidance and your will to succeed,
All is bound to turn out right!

                    ...Sheryl Santangelo

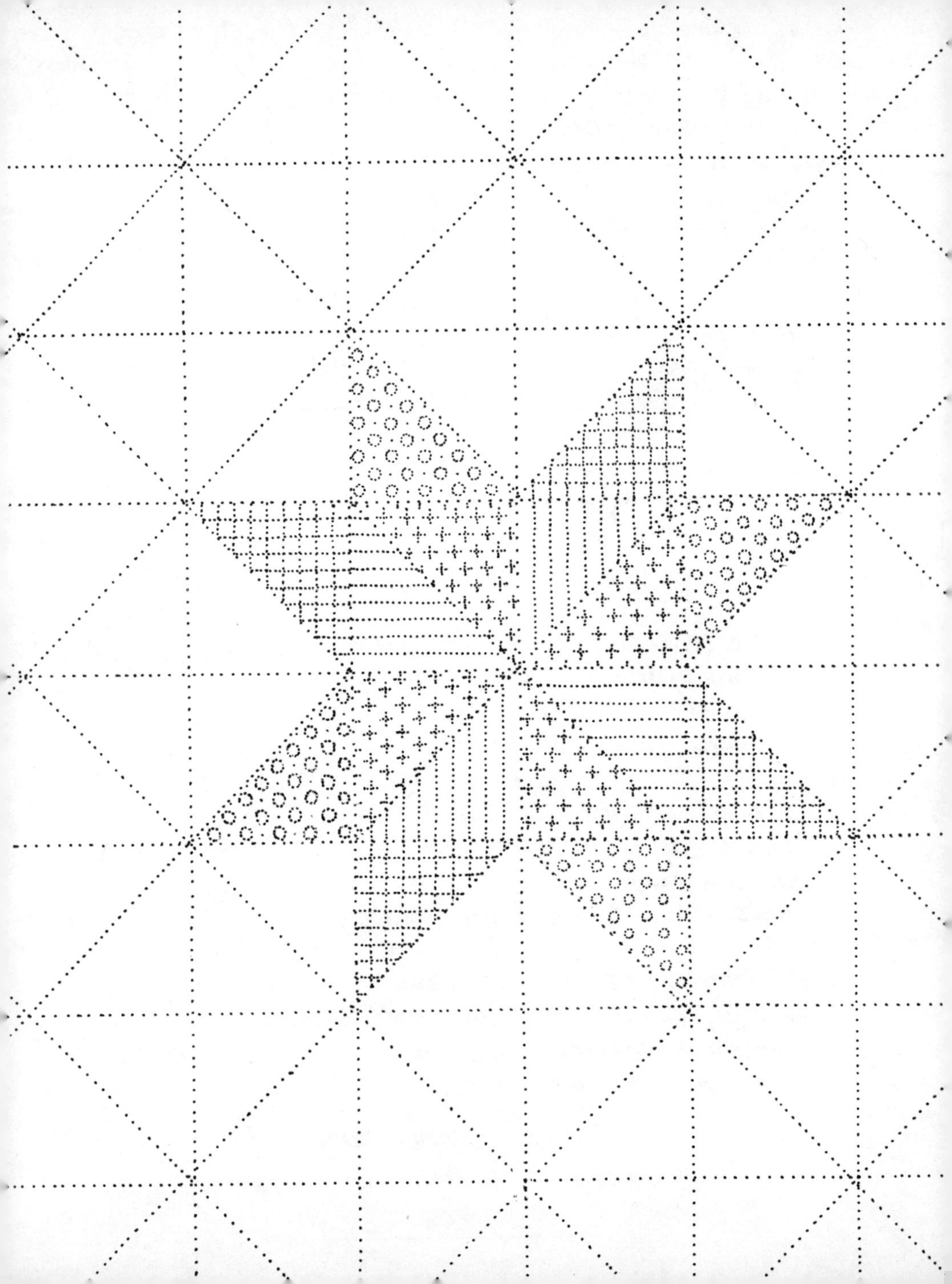

# Puddings, and everything else

Brown Rice Pudding ................................ 88
Fruit Kanten ............................................ 90
Chunky Applesauce ................................ 92
Peach Fool .............................................. 94
Baked Stuffed Apples ............................. 96
Squash Pudding ..................................... 98
Yucatan Yogurt Shake ............................ 99
Cream Cheese Icing ............................. 100
Wild Whipped Cream ........................... 101

serves 6 to 8

# Brown Rice Pudding

...hearty, delicious & down right transcendental!

- 2 cups raw brown rice
- 4 cups water
- 3 cups raw milk (pg. 105)
  (plus some extra for serving)
- 1½ cups honey
- 2 tsp. cinnamon
- 1 tsp. vanilla
- 1 cup raisins (optional)

Rinse rice well. Place in a large pot — pour in 4 cups water. Cover and bring to a boil. Lower flame and simmer 45 minutes. Then add 3 cups milk, and honey — cover

and continue to simmer... about 50 minutes. Add vanilla, raisins, and cinnamon. Stir well. Take off heat and let cool. Spoon into a bowl or individual serving bowls, and refrigerate ⌣ or... serve warm with extra milk. For those who like it sweeter, pass around some pure maple syrup. A sprinkle of chopped walnuts or almonds makes a nice addition. You could also pass around a small pitcher of ½ cream & ½ milk (better known as "Half 'n Half") to make it RICH, RICH, RICH!
..... You only live once ⌣ just don't make a habit of it!

## *Fruit Kanten*

↳ *a natural jello loved by all! Simple to make and low in calories... for those of us who are watching our weight, yet nonetheless still need "large-ish" portions of dessert, for our mental well-being!*

3 bars of Agar Agar (pg. 103)
   (weighing .5 oz. each)

1 gallon apple juice (do use the full-bodied unfiltered variety, & not the anemic type!
   Note: this recipe comes from our dear pal, Annie, who is presently in nursing school, and thus tends to describe everything in medical terms!)

1 lb. seedless green grapes

1½ cups peeled & sliced apples, pears or blueberries (or any combination of the above, or any fresh fruit in season)

2 tbsp. cinnamon

5 ice cubes

In a large pot, mix apple juice with cinnamon and begin to heat. Chop Agar-Agar into 2" pieces and put into hot juice. Mix well, then bring to a gentle boil, and boil 15 minutes — stirring often. Remove from heat... add ice cubes. Cut up fruit into bite-size pieces & add to juice. Pour it all into a large bowl and refrigerate 3 to 4 hours. After it has been chilled for 1 hr., stir well with a wooden spoon — as fruit tends to settle on the bottom.

# Chunky Applesauce

... very delicious ~ simple
... serve by itself or top with a good
    vanilla ice cream for a marvelous treat!
... also great with plain yogurt

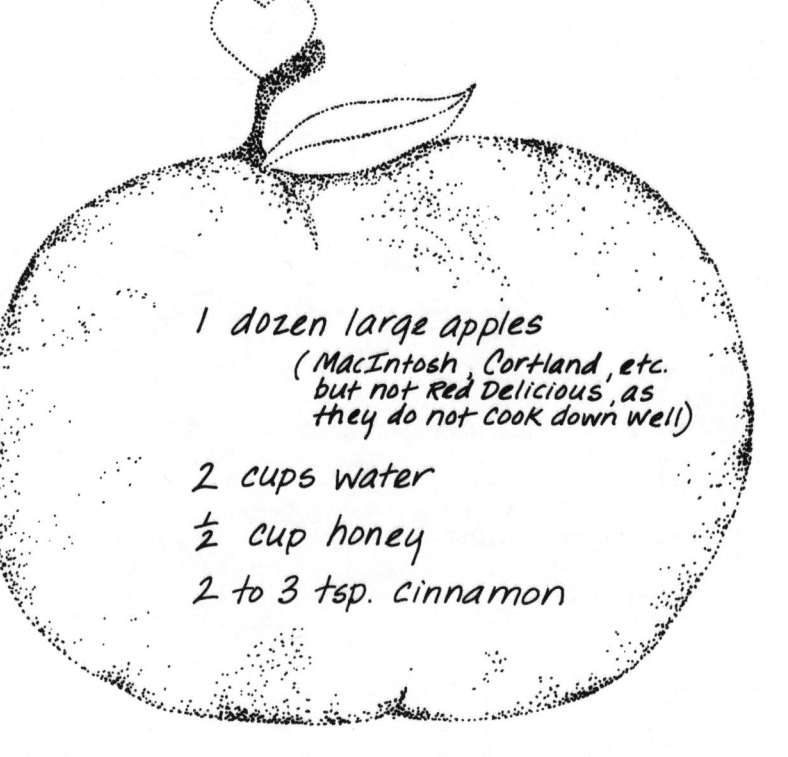

1 dozen large apples
   (MacIntosh, Cortland, etc.
   but not Red Delicious, as
   they do not cook down well)

2 cups water

½ cup honey

2 to 3 tsp. cinnamon

Peel, core and cut apples into large pieces. Put into a large pot — add water. Cover and bring to a boil. Reduce heat and simmer 20 minutes. Add honey and cinnamon. Mash apples with a potato masher. Let cool to room temperature, then refrigerate till chilled... or you can serve it warm with ice cream melting over it!

# Peach Fool

*a rich, creamy peach delight!*

*... thanks to Sharon*

- 2 cups fresh peaches (peeled & cut into small pieces)
- 2 tsp. cornstarch or arrowroot
- 1/2 cup honey
- 1/2 tsp. lemon juice
- 1/2 tsp. lemon rind (grated)
- 1 cup heavy cream
- 4 oz. cream cheese (softened)
- 1 tsp. vanilla
- 1/8 tsp. cinnamon
- a dash of nutmeg

Combine 1/4 c. honey, peaches, cornstarch, lemon juice and rind, cinnamon, and nutmeg in a pot. Bring to a boil, lower heat and cook until peaches are soft — about 5 minutes. Remove from heat & set aside to cool.

Meanwhile... combine 3 tbsp. cream, cream cheese, ¼ c. honey & 1 tsp. vanilla in a bowl and beat. Whip the cream till stiff — fold in the cream cheese mixture with the whipped cream, and then fold in the fruit mixture. Spoon into individual pudding bowls or parfait glasses, and chill a few hours before serving.

You can use BLUEBERRIES, STRAWBERRIES, RASPBERRIES, BLACK RASPBERRIES, Etc. Berries make the FOOL more colorful. Use 1 pint of berries & cook the fruit only 1 or 2 minutes, rather than the 5 minutes required for peaches.

serves 6

## Baked Stuffed Apples

*a very satisfying dessert, yet not too outrageously fattening!*

6 large apples (Winesap were used for this recipe)

½ cup chopped figs

½ cup chopped walnuts

½ cup raisins

3 tbsp. butter, melted

4 tbsp. honey

juice of 1 lemon

1 tsp. cinnamon

a pinch of mace  } optional
a pinch of nutmeg

Wash apples and carefully remove core, keeping the apple intact. Melt butter in a small pot on low heat — add honey, lemon juice and spices. Mix well. Chop figs and walnuts. Mix with raisins. Stuff core of apples with fig/nut mixture. Put apples into a baking dish. Spoon butter and honey mixture over and into core of apples. Bake at 350° for 45 minutes. Cool to room temperature, then chill.

... A NOTE TO THE <u>THIN</u> PEOPLE OF THE WORLD: This very slimming dessert can have a totally new dimension added to it by simply topping it with a "large-ish" <u>or</u> "smallish" scoop of vanilla ice cream!

# Squash Pudding

*a mad macro delight from Casey*

1 large butternut squash (peeled, seeded and cubed)
½ to ¾ cup water or apple juice
½ cup barley malt (pg. 107)
2 tbsp. sesame tahini (pg. 107)
1 tbsp. white miso (pg. 105)
½ tsp. vanilla
¼ cup chopped roasted nuts
pinch of sea salt

Place all ingredients except miso and nuts into a heavy pot. Let steam till squash is soft enough to mash with a potato masher or wire whisk. Blend in white miso & let cook on low flame for 5 min. Do not let miso boil. Serve warm or cool with a sprinkling of chopped nuts.

*serves 2 to 4*

# Yucatan Yogurt Shake

*... down right tropical!*

⌐from a little funky family-run restaurant on the Yucatan peninsula in Mexico.

Here is the original recipe, but use your imagination and try different fruits ⌐ even nuts can be blended in if you like.....

- 1 pint plain yogurt
- 2 ripe bananas
- 1 ripe mango
- 1 ripe papaya
- a little fresh pineapple (about ½ cup)
- 2 to 3 tbsp. honey

Put it all into a blender or food processor and whirl into a smooth, thick consistency. Pour into glasses and serve immediately... or chill till serving. Dust the top of the glass with a sprinkle of cinnamon.

⌐ the perfect summer breakfast... or a delicious healthy dessert!

# Cream Cheese Icing

...for carrot cake, banana bread, etc.
⌐ very simple!

8 oz. cream cheese
½ cup honey or maple syrup
1 tsp. vanilla
½ cup powdered milk (optional)
juice of 1 lemon

Soften cream cheese ⌐ mix well with honey, vanilla, powdered milk and lemon juice.

...You can squeeze an orange in the icing for a nice change ⌐ just eliminate the lemon... or try with a little of each.

...You could even mash strawberries, or other berries for a new flavor and neat color!

*enough for 8 people*

# Wild Whipped Cream

### or <u>BUTTER ICING</u>

... rich and natural !

1 cup heavy whipping cream
2 tbsp. maple syrup or honey

Pour the cream into a bowl ⁓ add maple syrup or honey ... and whip it !

... a little vanilla or a pinch of cinnamon or nutmeg can be added for a subtle flavor.

### <u>NOTE</u>:

Be careful not to overbeat the cream, or it could turn to butter. Now.... if that should happen, don't PANIC !! You have the basics of a good butter icing. Spread it on ⁓ use your imagination ..........
....... mash some berries in it for taste & color ⁓ maybe add a little more maple syrup or honey. Try a little carob powder (<u>not</u> with the berries!) for a carob butter icing.

⁓ it just goes to show you that there are no absolutes in cooking !!

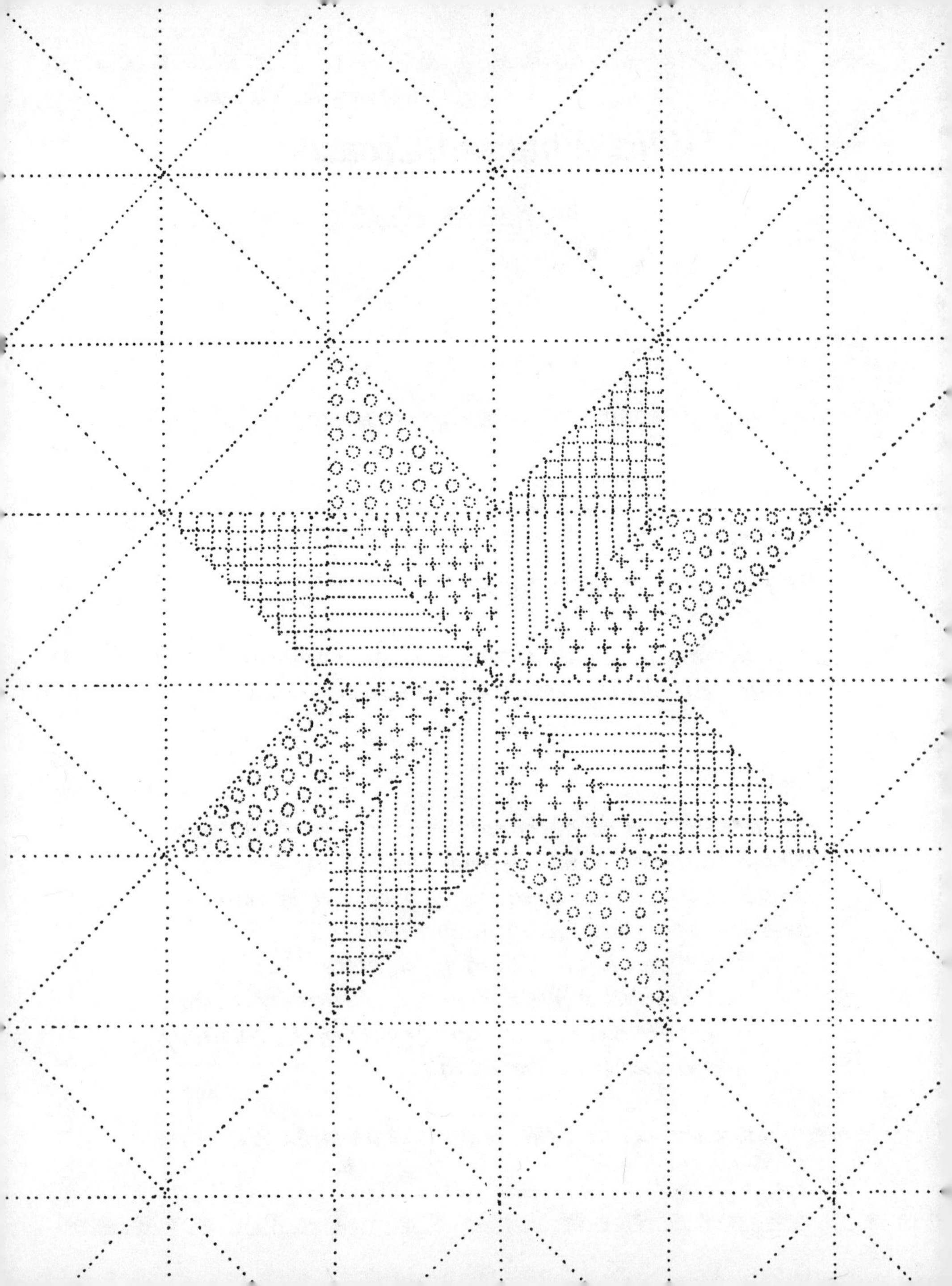

# *Glossary*

<u>Agar-Agar</u> – is a seaweed gelatin. Commercially sold gelatins are derived from animal sources. Agar-Agar is not only natural, it is also high in essential minerals. It is flavorless, so fruit and juice can be added to make desserts. Vegetables and vegetable juices can be added to make aspics.

<u>Arrowroot</u> (or Kuzu) – is a thickening agent used in place of cornstarch or flour. It is easily digested and is said to be good for stomach ailments.

<u>Baking Powder</u> – most baking powders contain alum, an aluminum compound. The body stores aluminum in the liver, lungs, thyroid, and brain, and in excess it can be toxic. You can purchase aluminum-free baking powder at health food stores.

<u>Butter vs. Margarine</u> – butter far surpasses margarine in taste, plus it lends the most delicate texture to pastries. Although butter has a high fat content, it contains vitamin E which helps reduce cholestrol. It also contains vitamin A and iodine. Margarine is hydrogenated in order to make it

solid, and this process creates fatty acids in it that are not found in nature. Also, it generally contains colorings and preservatives. All of this suggests that moderate use of butter may be far better than margarine in your diet.

<u>Carob vs. Chocolate</u> — chocolate is high in fat (and usually sugar). Many people are allergic to it, and it contains a caffeine-like alkaloid called theobromine that is believed to be addictive. Theobromine is also a heart stimulant and has been known to cause gastrointestinal trouble. Carob, on the other hand, has none of these shortcomings. It is nutritious, low in fats, and naturally sweet. (You can purchase unsweetened carob, or carob sweetened with sugar, date sugar or fructose.) The taste and texture of carob is very similar to chocolate.

<u>Filo Dough</u> — is a paper-thin dough that produces a flaky crust. It can be found at cheese and gourmet stores. Directions for use are on the box.

<u>Flour</u> — most of the desserts in this book are made with whole wheat pastry flour, which

is ground from soft spring wheat. The pastry flour has less gluten and protein in it than whole wheat flour (which is made from a hard, red winter wheat), and it has a more delicate flaky texture. Whole wheat pastry flour should be used for cakes and pastries, but not for yeasted breads, since breads need the higher gluten content of _regular_ whole wheat flour.

<u>Graham Crackers</u> — most health food stores carry graham crackers made with whole wheat flour and honey.

<u>Ice Cream</u> — there are several companies that make ice cream sweetened with honey or maple syrup. Look for them at health food stores.

<u>Milk</u> — pasteurization, in heating milk, destroys some of the vitamins and minerals. Therefore raw milk is considered superior. It can be purchased at health food stores.

<u>Miso</u> — is a concentrated paste made from fermented soybeans, rice, barley, or a combination of these. It is high in protein and imparts a delicious flavor to soups, sauces, dressings, etc.

<u>Oils</u> — <u>Safflower</u> and <u>Sunflower</u> are good, mild-tasting oils which can be used in baking. <u>Corn oil</u> is also good, yet stronger tasting than safflower and sunflower. Peanut oil is best for frying, since it can withstand high temperatures without burning.
Oils should be refrigerated to prevent rancidity. Use unrefined oils, since they possess their natural flavor, aroma and nutrients (particularly lecithin and vitamins A, E and K). Lecithin and vitamin E aid the body in reducing cholestrol build-up.

<u>Sweeteners</u> — It is common knowledge that refined sugar is not the best thing for ones health. There are several alternatives to sugar that not only taste better, but are also more nutritious.

<u>Honey</u> — raw honey is best. Heating destroys some of the vitamins and minerals. Some honey is stronger in flavor than others. Light tasting honey, such as clover or orange blossom is best for baking.

<u>Maple Syrup</u> — is <u>**wonderful**</u> for baking and desserts. It has a delicious and delicate flavor, and it is also good for you.

<u>Maple Syrup Granules</u> — are as sweet as

maple syrup, but similar to brown sugar in consistency. This makes it a wonderful substitute for sugar. The granules are formed by dehydrating maple syrup.

<u>Barley Malt</u> — extract is made from sprouted malt. It is an excellent sweetener. It is quite thick and concentrated, with a consistency like corn syrup and molasses.

<u>Molasses</u> — Sorghum molasses is the purest of the molasses available. It comes from sorghum, which is in the cereal grain family. Sulfured and Blackstrap molasses are by-products of the sugar cane and may contain impurities.

<u>Tahini</u> — is a nut butter made from hulled sesame seeds. It is rich in calcium and is a good source of protein. It also contains lecithin, phosphorus, iron, and vitamins B and E.

<u>Tapioca</u> — can be obtained at grocery and health food stores. It is a natural starch derived from the cassava plant.

..."Burnt Offerings"

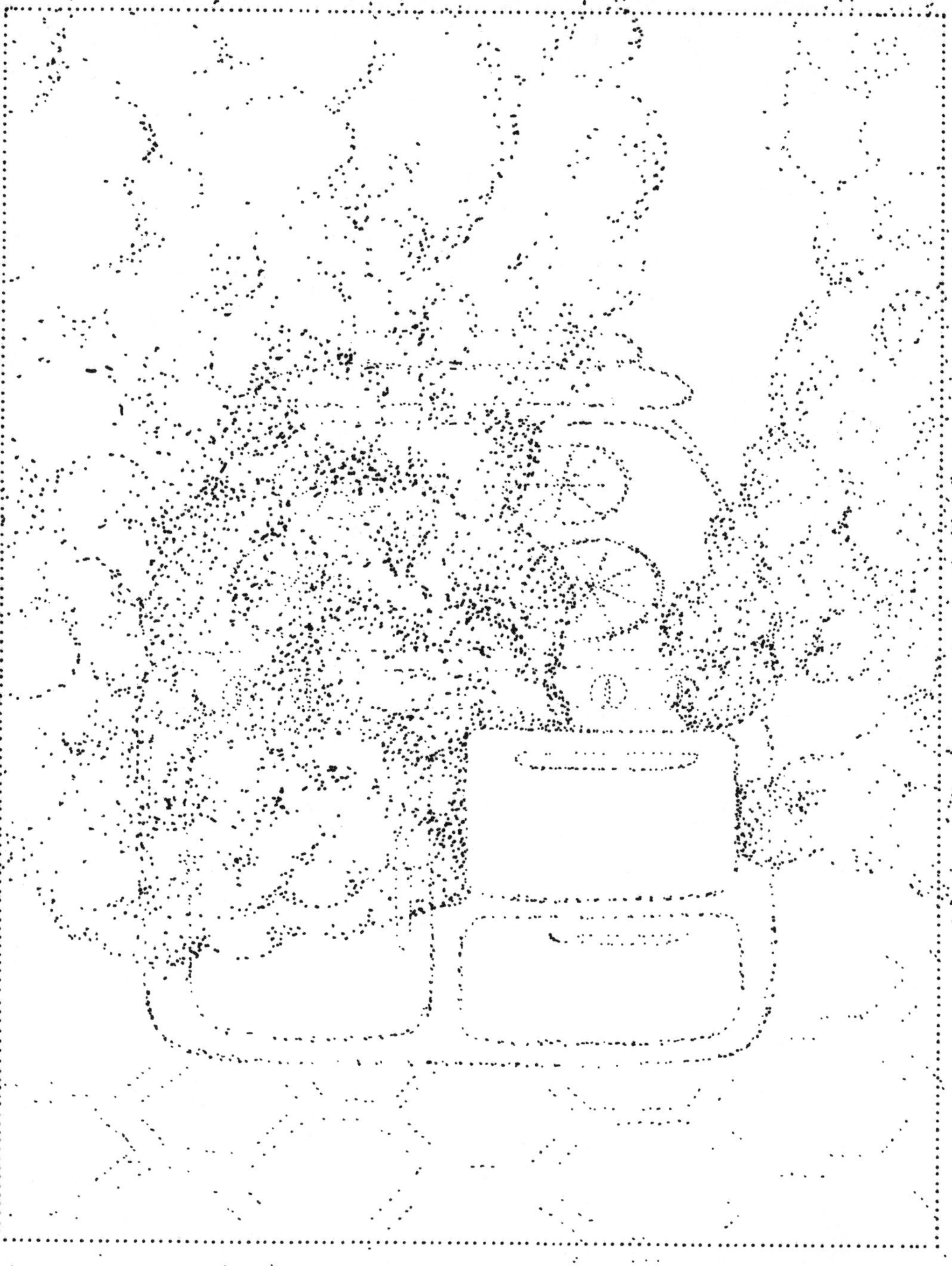

# *Index*

Agar Agar (see glossary) ............................................. 103
   fruit kanten ..................................................... 90
Almonds
   graham cracker nut crust ........................................ 81
   nutty oat crust ................................................. 82
Apple Walnut Cake ................................................... 58
Apple Walnut Crunch ................................................. 12
Apples
   baked stuffed ................................................... 96
   divine cream torte .............................................. 24
   pumpkin apple pie ............................................... 2
   walnut cake ..................................................... 58
   walnut crunch .................................................. 12
Arrowroot (see glossary) ............................................. 103

Baked stuffed apples ................................................. 96
Baking Powder (see glossary) ......................................... 103
Baklava .............................................................. 42
Banana
   chip muffins ................................................... 66
   nut muffins .................................................... 76
Banana Chip Muffins .................................................. 66
Banana Nut Muffins ................................................... 76
Barley Malt (see glossary) ........................................... 107
Blueberry
   creamy peach berry pie .......................................... 4
   crumble berry pie ............................................... 30
   honey glazed tart ............................................... 26
   nectar berry pie ................................................ 16
Blustery Day Oatmeal Cookies ......................................... 62
BROWNIES
   carob fudge .................................................... 40
   date nut chip .................................................. 48
Brown Rice Pudding ................................................... 88
Brown Rice ........................................................... 88

Butter (see glossary) .................................................. 103

CAKES
    apple walnut ..................................................... 58
    carrot ........................................................... 36
    old fashioned peach pear shortcake ............................... 44
    pineapple cheesecake ............................................ 52
    pumpkin ........................................................ 46
    simple spice .................................................... 54
    spicey pear ..................................................... 38

Carob (see glossary) ................................................... 104
Carob Chips
    banana chip muffins ............................................. 66
    carob fudge brownies ............................................ 40
    date nut chip brownies ........................................... 48
Carob Fudge Brownies .................................................. 40
Carrot Cake ............................................................ 36
Chocolate (see glossary) ............................................... 104
Chunky Applesauce ..................................................... 92
Cinnamon Buns, Deliciously Wholesome Whole Wheat ................. 78
COOKIES
    blustery day oatmeal ............................................. 62
Cranberries
    cranberry nut muffins ........................................... 68
Cranberry Nut Muffins .................................................. 68
Cream Cheese
    divine apple cream torte ......................................... 24
    icing ........................................................... 100
    mango mania .................................................... 28
    peach fool ...................................................... 94
    pineapple cheesecake ............................................ 52
    pumpkin cream pie .............................................. 8
    strawberry cream pie ............................................ 20
Cream Cheese Icing ................................................... 100
Creamy Peach Berry Pie ................................................. 4

Crumb Top Peach Pie .................................................. 18
Crumble Berry Pie .................................................... 30
CRUSTS
    graham cracker nut ............................................. 81
    nutty oat ...................................................... 82
    wonderfully whole wheaty pie ................................... 84

Date Nut Chip Brownies ............................................... 48
Date Nut Muffins ..................................................... 70
Dates
    nut chip brownies .............................................. 48
    nut muffins .................................................... 70
Deliciously Wholesome Whole Wheat Cinnamon Buns ...................... 78
Divine Apple Cream Torte ............................................. 24

Filo Dough (see glossary) ........................................... 104
    baklava ........................................................ 42
Flours (see glossary) ............................................... 104
Fruit Kanten ......................................................... 90

Gingerbread Muffins .................................................. 72
Glossary ............................................................ 103
Golden Corn Fritters ................................................. 74
Graham Cracker Nut Crust ............................................. 81
Graham Crackers (see glossary) ...................................... 105
    mango mania .................................................... 28
    nut crust ...................................................... 81

Heavy Cream
    peach fool ..................................................... 94
    wild whipped cream ............................................ 101
Honey (see glossary) ................................................ 106
Honey Dews ........................................................... 56
Honey Glazed Blueberry Tart .......................................... 26

Ice Cream (see glossary) .................................................. 105

Kanten, fruit ............................................................. 90

Maple Syrup (see glossary) ............................................... 106
Maple Syrup Granules (see glossary) ...................................... 106
Mango
    Mania ................................................................ 28
    yucatan yogurt shake ................................................. 99
Mango Mania .............................................................. 28
Margarine (see glossary) ................................................. 103
Milk (see glossary) ...................................................... 105
    brown rice pudding ................................................... 88
    peach cobbler ........................................................ 22
    peach pear shortcake ................................................. 44
    pineapple cheesecake ................................................. 52
Miso (see glossary) ...................................................... 105
Molasses (see glossary) .................................................. 107
MUFFINS
    banana chip .......................................................... 66
    banana nut ........................................................... 76
    cranberry nut ........................................................ 68
    date nut ............................................................. 70
    gingerbread .......................................................... 72

Nectar Berry Pie ......................................................... 16
Nutty Oat Crust .......................................................... 82

Oatmeal Cookies, Blustery Day ............................................ 62
Oils (see glossary) ..................................................... 106
Old Fashioned Peach Pear Shortcake ....................................... 44

PIES
    apple walnut crunch .................................................. 12

PIES, continued

    black raspberry crisp .................................................. 32
    creamy peach berry ................................................... 4
    crumb top peach ...................................................... 18
    crumble berry ......................................................... 30
    divine apple cream torte ............................................. 24
    honey glazed blueberry tart .......................................... 26
    mango mania ........................................................... 28
    nectar berry .......................................................... 16
    peach cobbler ......................................................... 22
    pecan ................................................................. 10
    pumpkin apple ......................................................... 2
    pumpkin cream ......................................................... 8
    punk-in ............................................................... 33
    sour cherry kuchen ................................................... 14
    strawberry cream ..................................................... 20
    strawberry rhubarb sublime ........................................... 6

Peach Cobbler ............................................................. 22
Peach Fool ................................................................ 94
Peaches
    creamy peach berry pie ............................................... 4
    crumb top peach pie .................................................. 18
    fruit kanten ......................................................... 90
    old fashioned peach pear shortcake ................................... 44
    peach cobbler ........................................................ 22
    peach fool ........................................................... 94
Pears
    old fashioned peach pear shortcake ................................... 44
    spicey pear cake ..................................................... 38
Pecan Pie ................................................................. 10
Pineapple Cheesecake ..................................................... 52
Poppy Seed Strudel ....................................................... 50
Prune Butter
    poppy seed strudel ................................................... 50

PUDDINGS
- brown rice .................................................. 88
- squash ..................................................... 98

Pumpkin
- apple pie ................................................... 2
- cake ....................................................... 46
- cream pie .................................................. 8
- punk-in pie ................................................ 33

Pumpkin Apple Pie ............................................ 2
Pumpkin Cake ................................................ 46
Pumpkin Cream Pie ........................................... 8
Punk-In Pie .................................................. 33

Raisins
- apple walnut cake .......................................... 58
- apple walnut crunch ........................................ 12
- baked stuffed apples ....................................... 96
- poppy seed strudel ......................................... 50
- schnecken .................................................. 60

Rhubarb
- strawberry sublime ......................................... 6

Schnecken .................................................... 60
Simple Spice Cake ............................................ 54
Sour Cherry Kuchen .......................................... 14

Sour Cream
- crumble berry pie .......................................... 30
- punk-in pie ................................................ 33
- schnecken .................................................. 60
- sour cherry kuchen ......................................... 14
- strawberry cream pie ....................................... 20

Spice Cake, simple ........................................... 54
Spicey Pear Cake ............................................. 38
Squash Pudding ............................................... 98

Strawberry
- cream pie .................................................. 20
- fruit kanten ................................................ 90
- rhubarb sublime ............................................ 6
- schnecken .................................................. 60

Strawberry Cream Pie ............................................ 20
Strawberry Rhubarb Sublime ..................................... 6
Strudel, Poppy Seed ............................................. 50
Sweeteners (see glossary) ...................................... 106

Tahini (see glossary) .......................................... 107
Tapioca (see glossary) ......................................... 107

Walnuts
- apple cake ................................................. 58
- apple crunch ............................................... 12
- baklava .................................................... 42
- banana nut muffins ......................................... 76
- cranberry nut muffins ...................................... 68
- data nut chip brownies ..................................... 48
- date nut muffins ........................................... 70
- graham cracker nut crust ................................... 81
- schnecken .................................................. 60

Wild Whipped Cream ............................................ 101
Wonderfully Whole Wheaty Pie Crust ............................. 84

Yeast
- deliciously wholesome whole wheat cinnamon buns ............ 78

Yogurt
- creamy peach berry pie ..................................... 4
- punk-in pie ................................................ 33
- sour cherry kuchen ......................................... 14
- yucatan shake .............................................. 99

Yucatan Yogurt Shake ........................................... 99

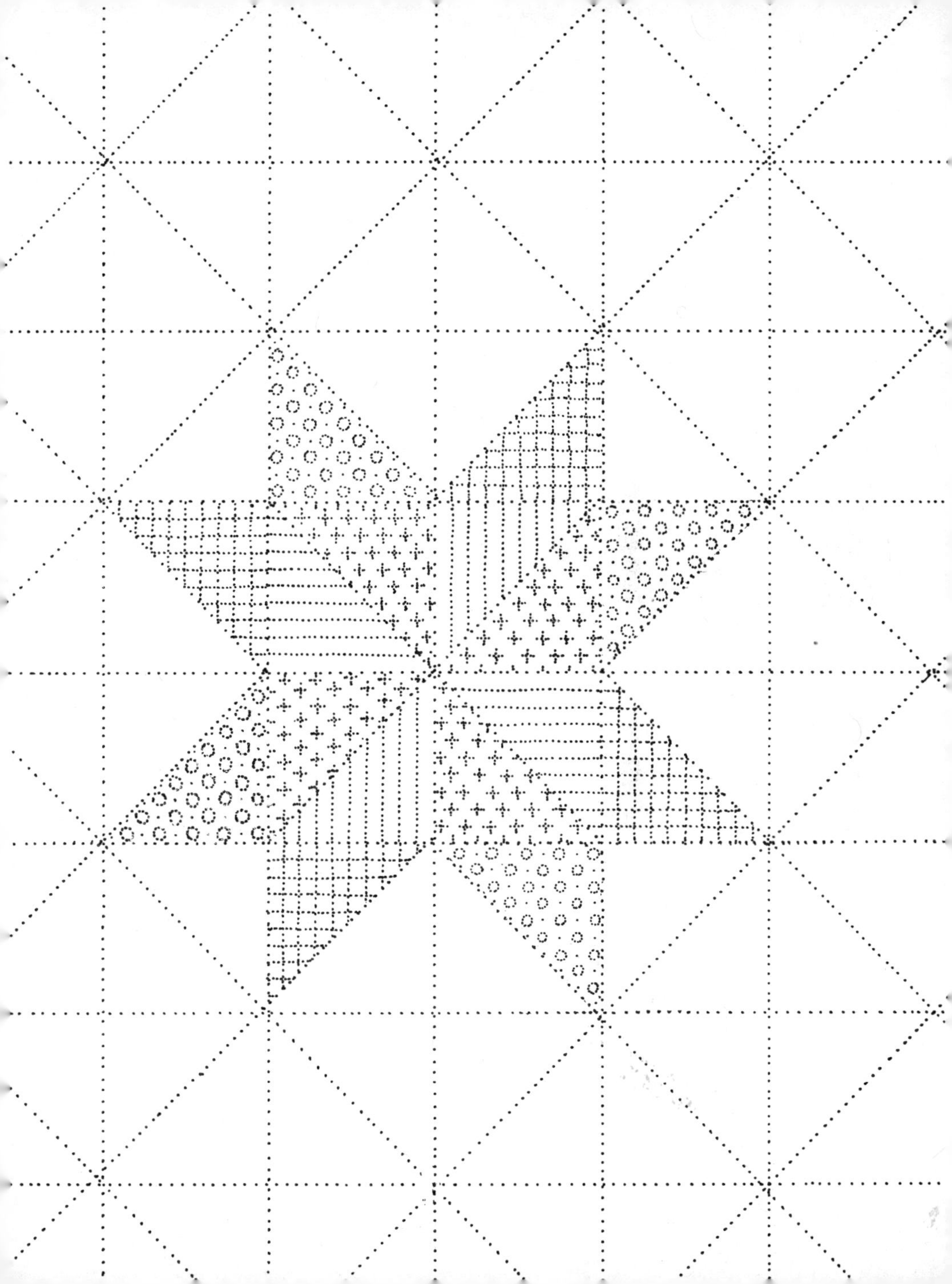